FUN STUFF FOR KIDS
AGES 7-9

FUN STUFF

FOR

KIDS

AGES 7-9

Michael Streff

ZondervanPublishingHouse

Grand Rapids, Michigan

A Division of HarperCollinsPublishers

Fun Stuff for Kids 7–9
Copyright © 1992 by Michael Streff

Requests for information should be addressed to:
Zondervan Publishing House
Grand Rapids, Michigan 49530

ISBN 0-310-57801-9

Edited by Diane Brummel Bloem
Illustrations by Michael Streff
Cover design by Terry Dugan Design

Printed in the United States of America

92 93 94 95 96 / ML / 10 9 8 7 6 5 4 3 2 1

CONTENTS

HELLO!

Welcome to "Fun Stuff for Kids 7-9"

IT'S FULL OF PUZZLES, QUIZZES AND ALL SORTS OF BRAIN TEASERS! GRAB A PENCIL, PUT YOUR BRAIN IN GEAR AND LET'S GO! DON'T FORGET YOUR BIBLES – YOU'LL NEED AN "NIV" TRANSLATION.

IT'S OKAY TO PHOTOCOPY THESE PAGES FOR CLASSROOM OR HOME USE. HERE ARE A FEW WAYS TO USE THEM:

 CHOOSE PUZZLES THAT TIE IN WITH YOUR SUNDAY SCHOOL LESSONS.

 RAINY DAY ACTIVITIES! CHASE AWAY SUMMER VACATION BLUES!

 HOME BIBLE STUDY!

CHAPTER 1
TRY THIS TRIVIA!

HOW MUCH DO YOU KNOW ABOUT THE BIBLE? FIND OUT! SEE HOW MANY QUESTIONS YOU CAN ANSWER WITHOUT LOOKING IN THE BIBLE, TEST YOUR SMARTS **AND** LEARN SOME NEW, NEAT BIBLE FACTS!

REMEMBER

NIV BIBLE

- TRIVIA QUIZZES:
  1. THE BIRTH OF JESUS!
  2. SLEEPERS
  3. MIRACLES OF JESUS
  4. CARING FOR OTHERS
  5. JESUS ON THE CROSS

ALL BIBLICAL REFERENCES IN THE PUZZLES ARE TO THE <u>NEW INTERNATIONAL VERSION</u> (NIV) OF THE BIBLE.

THE Birth of Jesus!

Matthew 2 and Luke 2

1. Bethlehem

Why did Joseph and Mary go to Bethlehem?

2. Why was Jesus laid in a manger?

3. The Name Book

Who named Jesus?

4. What gifts did the Magi bring to Jesus?

5.

6. Who told the shepherds that Jesus had been born?

Who sent the Magi (Wise Men) to find the baby Jesus?

7. Name the lady prophet who thanked God when she saw the baby Jesus.

Miracles of Jesus

③ Why did 4 men make a hole in a roof to see Jesus? (Mark 2:1-5)

② At a wedding feast, what did Jesus change into wine? (John 2:1-10)

① Which disciple did Jesus let walk on water? (Matthew 14:29)

⑤ How did Jesus heal the man who was blind from birth? (John 9:6)

④ How many loaves of bread were used to feed the 5,000? (John 6:9)

⑥ How was Jesus able to help Lazarus? (John 11:43-44)

Caring for Others

① If we obey God's commandments, how should we treat our mother and father? Exodus 20:12

② Name the Old Testament woman who picked grain for her mother-in-law. Ruth 2:17-18

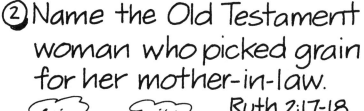

③ Who loves a cheerful giver? 2 Corinthians 9:7

To the needy

To the sick

To the poor

④ How will people know that we are disciples of Jesus? John 13:35

Hi! I'm a disciple

⑤ How should we treat our enemies? Luke 6:27

WE WON'T PLAY WITH YOU!

HEY STUPID!

LOOK AT HER FUNNY HAIR!

CHEF

⑥ If we fix a big dinner, whom should we invite to eat it? Luke 14:13-14

13

CHAPTER 2

WORD JUMBLES

FIRST, UNSCRAMBLE THE JUMBLED LETTERS TO FORM 5 WORDS. THEN ARRANGE THE CIRCLED LETTERS TO MAKE THE ANSWER TO THE QUESTION.

① DAVID AND GOLIATH • TEMPTATION OF JESUS
② SOLOMON • ELIJAH
③ HOW TO PRAY
④ ABSALOM
⑤ A WRESTLING MATCH!

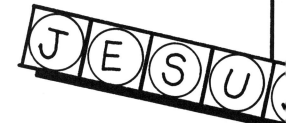

CODES

EACH OF THESE PUZZLES USES A CODE TO HELP YOU ANSWER QUESTIONS OR FINISH A BIBLE VERSE. FIND THE LETTERS YOU NEED IN THE CODE BOXES ON THE BOTTOM OF EACH PAGE.

① WHO IS JESUS?
② A NET FULL OF FISH
③ JESUS PRAYED
④ BUILDING BARNS
⑤ JERICHO!
⑥ BLESSINGS

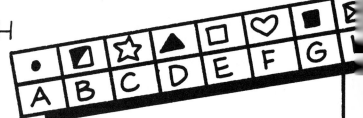

I SAMUEL 17:38-51

GNILS   ▢▢▢▢◯ (1)

RDOSW   ▢▢◯▢◯ (2) (3)

YARM   ▢◯▢▢ (4)

LODR   ▢◯▢▢ (5)

CKITS   ▢▢▢◯◯ (6) (7)

Who and what beat Goliath?

◯◯◯ and a ◯◯◯◯ !
1 2 3   4 5 6 7

LUKE 4:1-13

EKSTRI   ◯◯◯▢◯▢ (1)(2)(3) (6)

ENOST   ▢◯◯▢ (9)(7)

LULF   ▢◯▢▢ (8)

RUOY   ▢▢◯▢ (4)

BEOMCE   ▢▢◯▢▢▢ (5)

The devil tempted Jesus 3 times but he...

◯◯◯◯◯◯   ◯◯◯ !
1 2 3 4 5 6   7 8 9

I KINGS 3:5-14

RWONG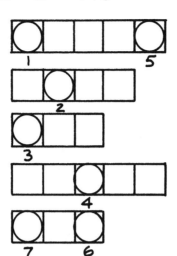

GINK

NOS

MEARD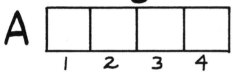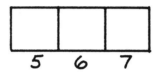

UYO

What King Solomon wanted to be:

A [1][2][3][4] [5][6][7]

I KINGS 17:1-6

BAHA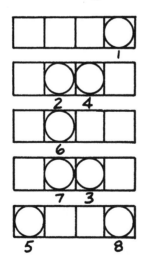

EIDH

RLOD

DROW

EEFD

What Elijah ate:

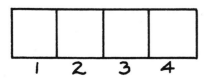 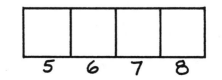

[1][2][3][4] [5][6][7][8]

How To Pray...

In Matthew 6:9-13 Jesus told his disciples how to pray. To finish the prayer, unscramble the words and write them in the matching shapes.

Our Father in ☐☐☐,
hallowed be your ⬗⬗,
your kingdom ⬗⬗,
your ⬡ be done
on ⬗ as it is in heaven.
Give us today our daily ⬯.
Forgive us our ⬭,
as we also have forgiven our debtors.
And ☐ us not into temptation,
but deliver us from the ⬗ one.

hreta   heanev   lliw

enam   dreab   lvei

emoc   deal   stedb

ABSALOM

Read about Absalom and David in 2 Samuel 15:1-18:18.

Unscramble the words in the story below. Use the clues in the pictures. (Correct answers are below.)

dvaiD ruled over Israel. His son Asalbom wanted to be gink. Absalom turned the people against David.

David flet Jerusalem. He was araidf of Absalom. David was very das. David and his family crossed the dserte.

Absalom followed David. They fought a great ttleab in the sterof. The army of Absalom was beaten.

Absalom rode a mleu. It ran under an koa tree. Absalom was caught by his raih. He was killed by boaJ. The battle stopped.

A Wrestling Match!

Read about Jacob in Genesis 32:22-32

Unscramble the words in the story below. Use the clues in the pictures. (Correct answers are below.)

coJab was on his way to see his rethrbo Esau. He was afraid Esau would kattac him.

Jacob prayed to oGd for help. Jacob sent gfits to Esau. He gave him sowc, slacme and oatgs.

At the rierv, Jacob wrestled with a nam. They wrestled all tginh. Jacob skade to be blessed.

The man bledsse Jacob and changed his enam to Israel. Jacob wenk that he had wrestled with God!

knew God brother attack river asked camels
blessed name Jacob cows man night gifts goats

19

WHO IS JESUS?

What does the Bible say about Jesus? Use the code to find the words that tell about our Savior.

Jesus is a...

Matthew 4:24

Acts 5:31

Jesus is...

Revelation 19:16

Matthew 4:23

John 9:39

Hebrews 5:8-9

Jesus brings...

John 1:17

John 1:17

Code:

A	C	D	E	F	G	H	I	J	K	L	M	N	O	P	R	S	T	U	V

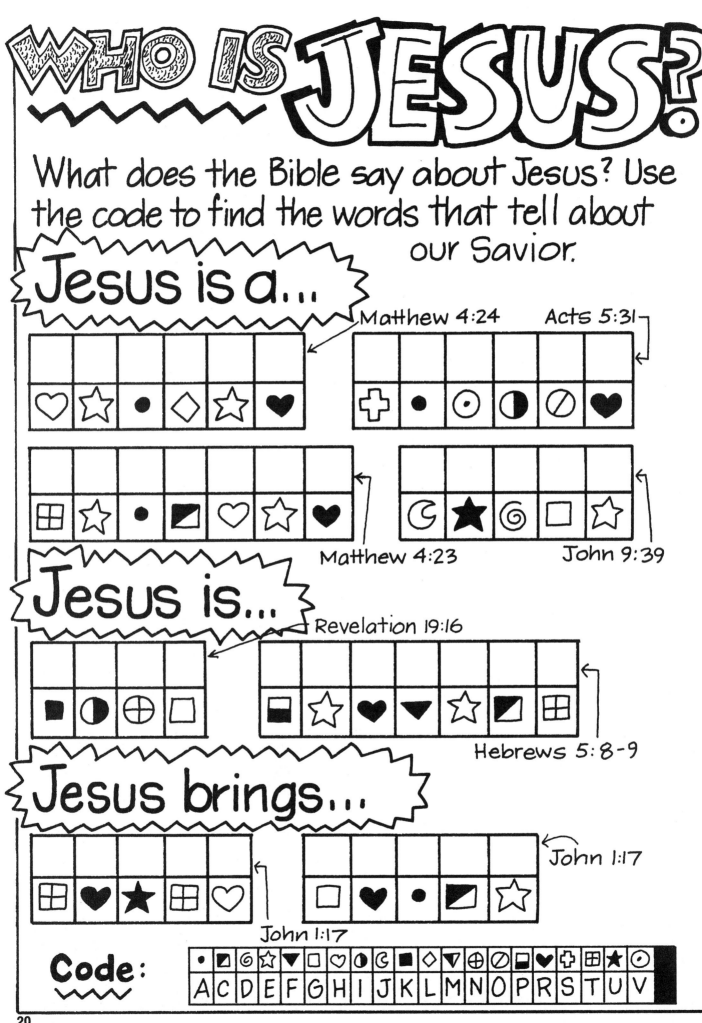

A NET FULL OF FISH

Why is the kingdom of Heaven like a net full of many kinds of fish?

Use the code below to finish the answer:

☐☐☐☐☐☐ will divide the

☐☐☐ ☐☐☐☐ ☐☐☐ ☐☐☐☐.

The ☐☐ will be thrown into

☐ ☐☐☐☐☐ ☐☐☐☐☐☐☐.

Matthew 13:47-50

A	B	C	D	E	F	G	H	I	K	L	M	N	O	R	S	T	U	V	W	Y

JESUS PRAYED

ALL OVER THE PLACE!

Use the code to find out where Jesus prayed.

1. In the ⬚⬚⬚⬚⬚ before he called his disciples. (Luke 6:12-13)

2. At the ⬚⬚⬚⬚ of Lazarus. (John 11:41-42)

3. On the ⬚⬚⬚⬚⬚. (Luke 23:34)

4. At the ⬚⬚⬚⬚⬚ before a meal. (Luke 24:28-31)

5. In the ⬚⬚⬚⬚⬚ ⬚⬚⬚⬚, before the "Lord's Supper." (Luke 22:14-18)

6. When he was baptized in the ⬚⬚⬚⬚⬚. (Luke 3:21)

a	b	c	e	g	h	i	l	m	n	o	p	r	s	t	u	v
○	⊙	●	⊕	◗	◖	⊖	⊙	⊡	☺	⊗	◎	÷	◉	■	▲	⊠

22

Building Barns

Use the code below to find the meaning of this parable.

Luke 12:15-21

Jesus tells us:

CODE

CODE

a	c	d	e	f	g	h	i	l	n	o	s	t	u	v	w

JERICHO!

Joshua 6:15-20

God promised Joshua victory over Jericho. Use the code to find out God's battle plan:

On the [☆][♥][⊖][♥][☽][★][□] (seventh) day,

[♥][▲][◇][●][□] (march) around the city 7 times. Have the 7 [⊕][◇][◨][♥][☆][★][☆] (priests) blow their [★][◇][✕][♥][⊕][♥][★][☆] (trumpets).

Have the people [☆][□][▽][✕][★] (shout). The walls will [★][✕][♡][○][⊠][♥] (tumble) down!

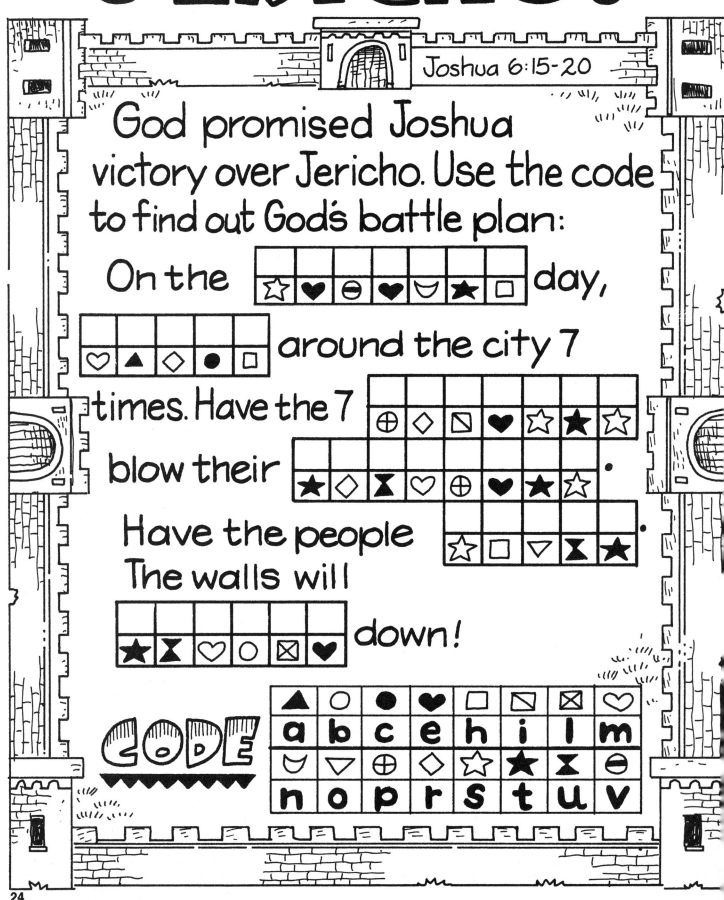

CODE

▲	○	●	♥	□	◨	⊠	♡
a	b	c	e	h	i	l	m
☽	▽	⊕	◇	☆	★	✕	⊖
n	o	p	r	s	t	u	v

BLESSINGS

In Matthew 5:3-12 Jesus blesses all his disciples. Use the code to discover the blessings he gives us!

Disciples who are...

Receive this blessing...

Poor in spirit... ▶ the kingdom of

7	4	1	14	4	9

Mournful (sad) ... ▶

2	10	8	5	10	11	13

Merciful... ▶

8	4	11	2	16

Pure in heart... ▶ will see

6	10	3

Peacemakers... ▶ will be called

12	10	9	12

of God.

Insulted because of their faith... ▶ a reward in

7	4	1	14	4	9

CODE

a	c	d	e	f	g	h	m	n	o	r	s	t	v	w	y
1	2	3	4	5	6	7	8	9	10	11	12	13	14	15	16

CHAPTER 3

WORD SEARCH

TO SOLVE THESE PUZZLES, YOU WILL TRY TO FIND WORDS HIDDEN IN THE SQUARES OF LETTERS. THE WORDS YOU NEED TO FIND ARE LISTED AROUND EACH PUZZLE.

① KINGS WHO RULED JUDAH
② CLOTHES
③ FOOD
④ NAMES
⑤ TREES
⑥ BIRDS
⑦ ANIMALS

CROSSWORD PUZZLES

IN EACH OF THE CROSSWORD PUZZLES, YOU NEED TO COMPLETE BIBLE VERSES OR ANSWER A QUESTION AND FILL IN THE BLANK SQUARES. USE YOUR BIBLE TO FIND THOSE WORDS YOU DON'T KNOW.

① JESUS IS BORN
② IN THE LION'S DEN
③ PARTING THE SEA
④ CREATION
⑤ ONE MEAL THAT FED 5,000
⑥ THE GOOD NEIGHBOR
⑦ TAX MAN IN A TREE
⑧ JACOB'S DREAM

KINGS WHO RULED JUDAH

There are 11 kings hidden in the puzzle.
See if you can find all of them!

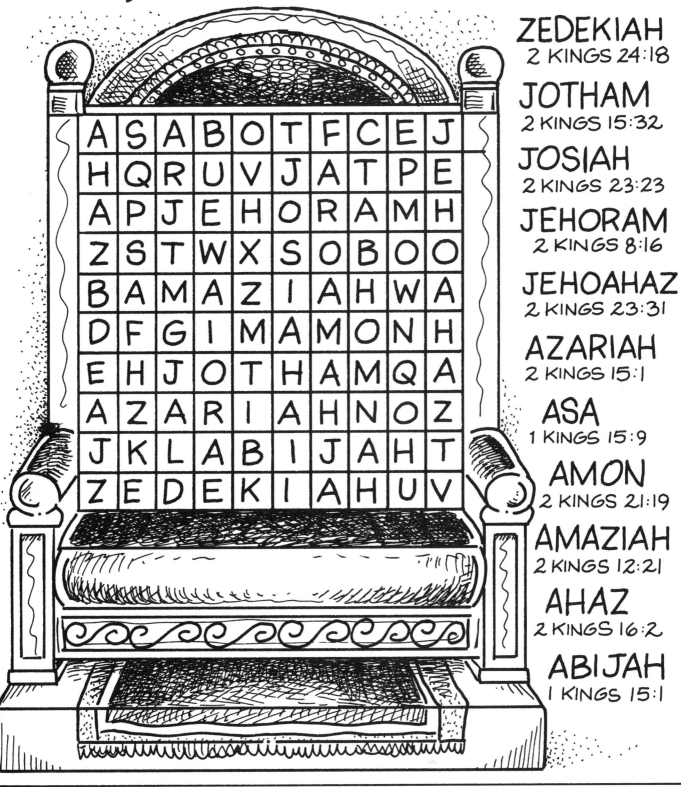

A	S	A	B	O	T	F	C	E	J
H	Q	R	U	V	J	A	T	P	E
A	P	J	E	H	O	R	A	M	H
Z	S	T	W	X	S	O	B	O	O
B	A	M	A	Z	I	A	H	W	A
D	F	G	I	M	A	M	O	N	H
E	H	J	O	T	H	A	M	Q	A
A	Z	A	R	I	A	H	N	O	Z
J	K	L	A	B	I	J	A	H	T
Z	E	D	E	K	I	A	H	U	V

ZEDEKIAH
2 KINGS 24:18

JOTHAM
2 KINGS 15:32

JOSIAH
2 KINGS 23:23

JEHORAM
2 KINGS 8:16

JEHOAHAZ
2 KINGS 23:31

AZARIAH
2 KINGS 15:1

ASA
1 KINGS 15:9

AMON
2 KINGS 21:19

AMAZIAH
2 KINGS 12:21

AHAZ
2 KINGS 16:2

ABIJAH
1 KINGS 15:1

Clothes

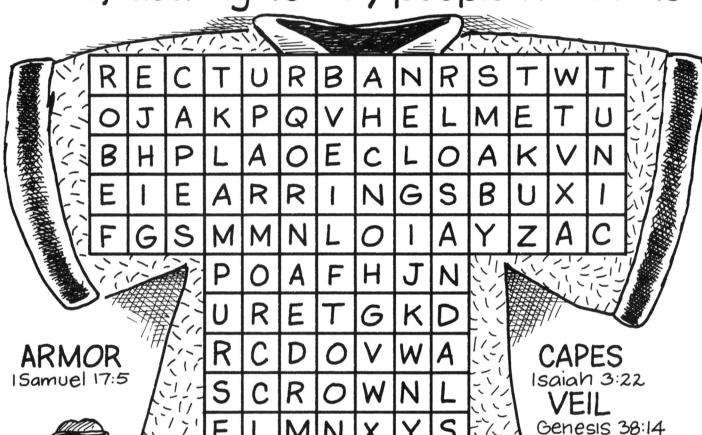

See if you can find the **13** articles of clothing worn by people in the Bible.

R	E	C	T	U	R	B	A	N	R	S	T	W	T
O	J	A	K	P	Q	V	H	E	L	M	E	T	U
B	H	P	L	A	O	E	C	L	O	A	K	V	N
E	I	E	A	R	R	I	N	G	S	B	U	X	I
F	G	S	M	M	N	L	O	I	A	Y	Z	A	C
		P	O	A	F	H	J	N					
		U	R	E	T	G	K	D					
		R	C	D	O	V	W	A					
		S	C	R	O	W	N	L					
		E	L	M	N	X	Y	S					
		S	H	A	W	L	S	A					

ARMOR
1 Samuel 17:5

CAPES
Isaiah 3:22
VEIL
Genesis 38:14

CLOAK
Acts 12:8

ROBE
Exodus 28:31

CROWN
2 Samuel 1:10

SANDALS
Acts 12:8

EARRINGS
Isaiah 3:19

SHAWLS
Isaiah 3:23

HELMET
1 Samuel 17:5

TURBAN
Exodus 28:37

PURSES
Isaiah 3:22

TUNIC
Exodus 28:39

FOOD

You will find **11** kinds of food hidden in the basket below:

STEW
Genesis 25:29

CAKES
Exodus 12:39

GRAIN
1 Samuel 25:18

MILK
Exodus 3:8

HONEY
2 Samuel 17:29

RAISINS
1 Samuel 25:18

CHEESE
2 Samuel 17:29

Z	H	O	N	E	Y	X	Z	C	F
O	N	I	O	N	S	F	I	S	H
R	A	I	S	I	N	S	O	U	B
B	F	K	P	O	C	A	K	E	S
T	C	H	E	E	S	E	O	Z	W
Z	S	Q	C	T	B	E	A	N	S
M	E	L	O	N	S	B	G	H	R
H	J	K	Z	P	O	M	I	L	K
G	R	A	I	N	Z	O	B	Q	U
A	C	E	L	O	Y	S	T	E	W

BEANS
2 Samuel 17:28

FISH
John 6:9

MELONS
Numbers 11:5

ONIONS
Numbers 11:5

NAMES

See if you can find 12 Bible names in the book!

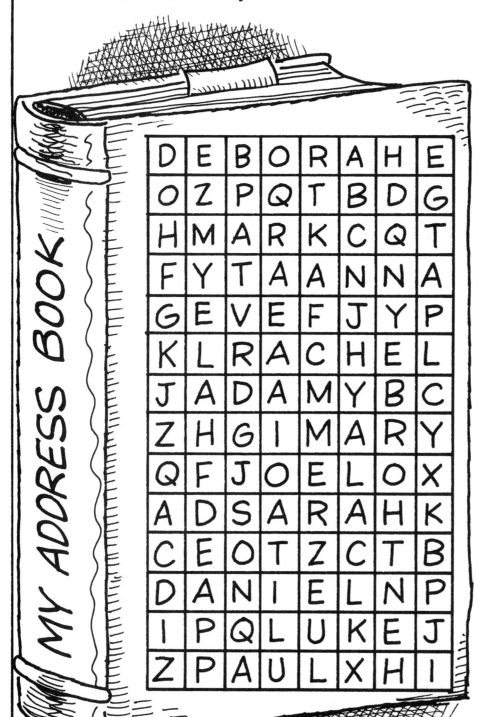

ADAM
(Red earth)
ANNA
(Grace)
DANIEL
(God is judge)
DEBORAH
(Bee)
EVE
(Life)
JOEL
(The Lord is God)
LUKE
(Light-giving)
MARK
(Polite)
MARY
(Bitterness)
PAUL
(Little)
RACHEL
(Ewe)
SARAH
(Queen)

TREES

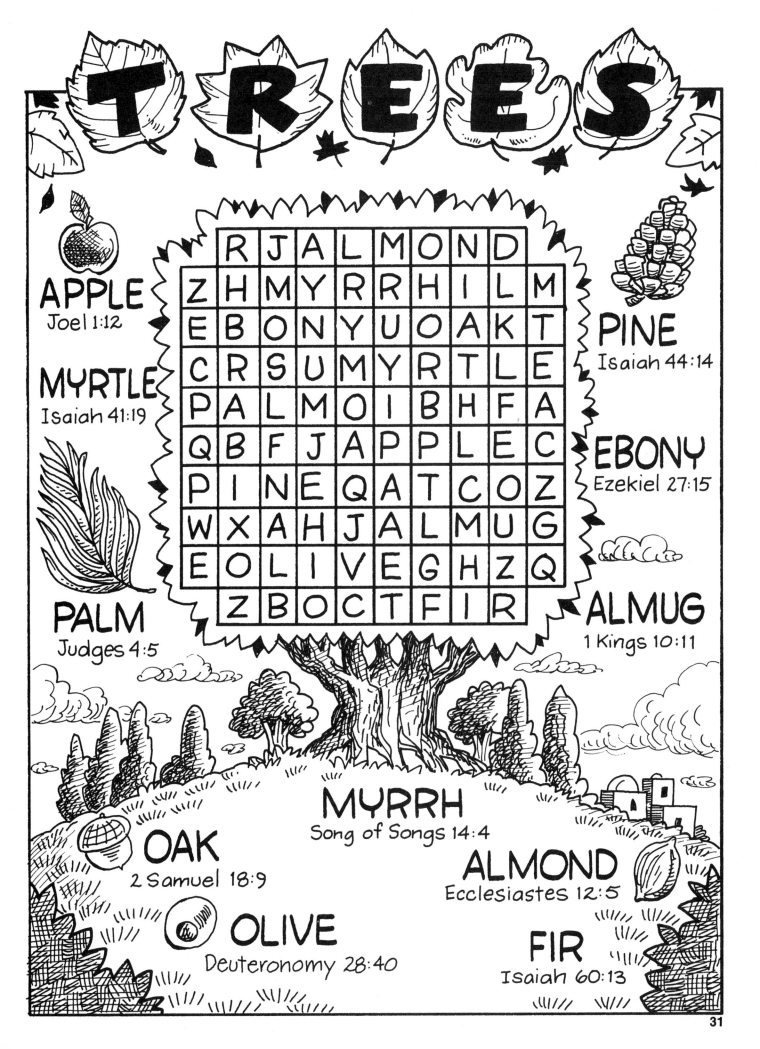

APPLE
Joel 1:12

MYRTLE
Isaiah 41:19

PALM
Judges 4:5

PINE
Isaiah 44:14

EBONY
Ezekiel 27:15

ALMUG
1 Kings 10:11

MYRRH
Song of Songs 14:4

OAK
2 Samuel 18:9

OLIVE
Deuteronomy 28:40

ALMOND
Ecclesiastes 12:5

FIR
Isaiah 60:13

R	J	A	L	M	O	N	D	
Z	H	M	Y	R	R	H	I	L	M
E	B	O	N	Y	U	O	A	K	T
C	R	S	U	M	Y	R	T	L	E
P	A	L	M	O	I	B	H	F	A
Q	B	F	J	A	P	P	L	E	C
P	I	N	E	Q	A	T	C	O	Z
W	X	A	H	J	A	L	M	U	G
E	O	L	I	V	E	G	H	Z	Q
Z	B	O	C	T	F	I	R		

31

Birds

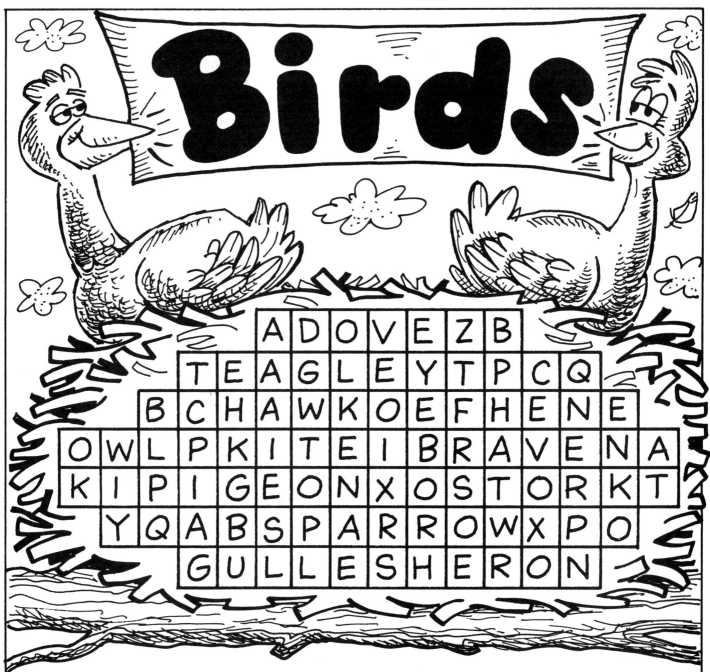

A	D	O	V	E	Z	B				
T	E	A	G	L	E	Y	T	P	C	Q
B	C	H	A	W	K	O	E	F	H	E	N	E
O	W	L	P	K	I	T	E	I	B	R	A	V	E	N	A
K	I	P	I	G	E	O	N	X	O	S	T	O	R	K	T
Y	Q	A	B	S	P	A	R	R	O	W	X	P	O
G	U	L	L	E	S	H	E	R	O	N

Find the 12 birds in the nest above.

DOVE
Isaiah 38:14

HEN
Luke 13:34

HERON
Leviticus 11:19

HAWK
Job 39:26

EAGLE
Deuteronomy 32:11

OWL
Isaiah 34:15

RAVEN
Proverbs 30:17

SPARROW
Proverbs 26:2

PIGEON
Genesis 15:9

STORK
Leviticus 11:19

KITE
Leviticus 11:14

GULL
Leviticus 11:16

ANIMALS

Can you find all **13** of the animals hidden on the ark below?

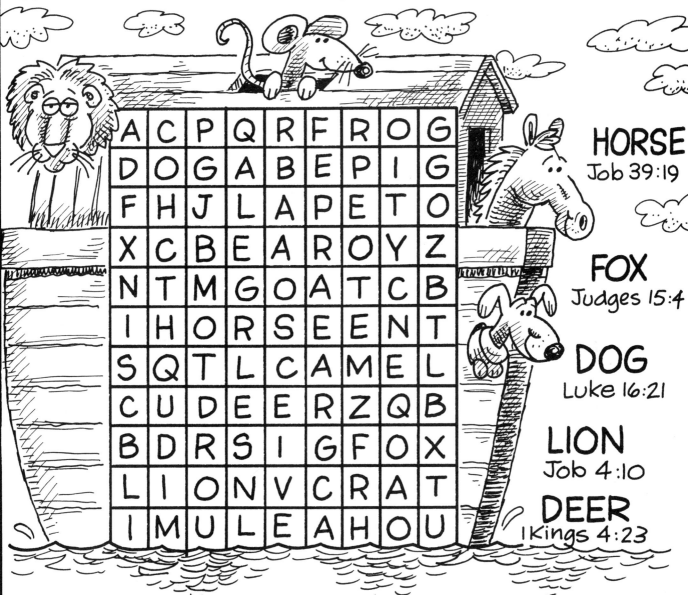

A	C	P	Q	R	F	R	O	G
D	O	G	A	B	E	P	I	G
F	H	J	L	A	P	E	T	O
X	C	B	E	A	R	O	Y	Z
N	T	M	G	O	A	T	C	B
I	H	O	R	S	E	E	N	T
S	Q	T	L	C	A	M	E	L
C	U	D	E	E	R	Z	Q	B
B	D	R	S	I	G	F	O	X
L	I	O	N	V	C	R	A	T
I	M	U	L	E	A	H	O	U

HORSE Job 39:19

FOX Judges 15:4

DOG Luke 16:21

LION Job 4:10

DEER I Kings 4:23

MULE I Kings 1:33

PIG Mark 5:13

GOAT Luke 15:29

FROG Psalm 78:45

BEAR 2 Samuel 17:8

CAMEL Genesis 32:15

RAT Isaiah 66:17

APE I Kings 10:22

JESUS IS BORN

Read about the baby Jesus in Luke 2:1-40

Across

① There was no room at the _____ . verse 7

③ The shepherds saw an _____ . verse 9

④ Mary wrapped the _____ in cloths. verses 6,7

⑦ Joseph belonged to the _____ and line of David. verse 4

⑧ The angel told them about the birth of _____ . verse 11

Down

② Joseph and Mary lived in _____ . verse 4

⑤ Anna thanked _____ when she saw Jesus. verse 38

⑥ Simeon _____ the baby Jesus and his parents. verse 34

IN THE LION'S DEN

Read about Daniel and the lions in Daniel 6.

Across

① The king was unhappy that_____ broke the law. verse 14

⑤ Daniel worked for King _____ , verses 1,2

⑥ The king could not eat or_____ . verse 18

⑧ An _____ saved Daniel. verse 22

⑩ Daniel _____ in God. verse 23

Down

② Daniel prayed three _____ a day. verse 10

③ The men threw Daniel into the ___ den. verse 16

④ No one could _____ to God. verse 7

⑦ God was able to _____ Daniel. verse 20

⑨ Daniel was ___ hurt. verse 22

⑪ Darius told everyone to worship ___ . verse 26

PARTING THE SEA

Exodus 13:21-14:31

ACROSS

④ God was hidden in a _____ . 13:21

⑥ Moses told the people that God would _____ for them. 14:14

⑦ God told _____ to lead the people. 14:15

⑧ The Egyptians caught up with the Israelites _____ Pi Hahiroth. 14:9

⑨ The people _____ to the Lord. 14:10

⑪ _____ covered the Egyptian army. 14:28

⑫ The people put their _____ in God. 14:31

DOWN

① The Israelites did not want to die in the _____ . 14:11

② The people walked on dry _____ . 14:22

③ God used a strong _____ . 14:21

⑤ The Egyptians rode in their _____ . 14:9

⑩ The army of _____ chased the Israelites. 14:23

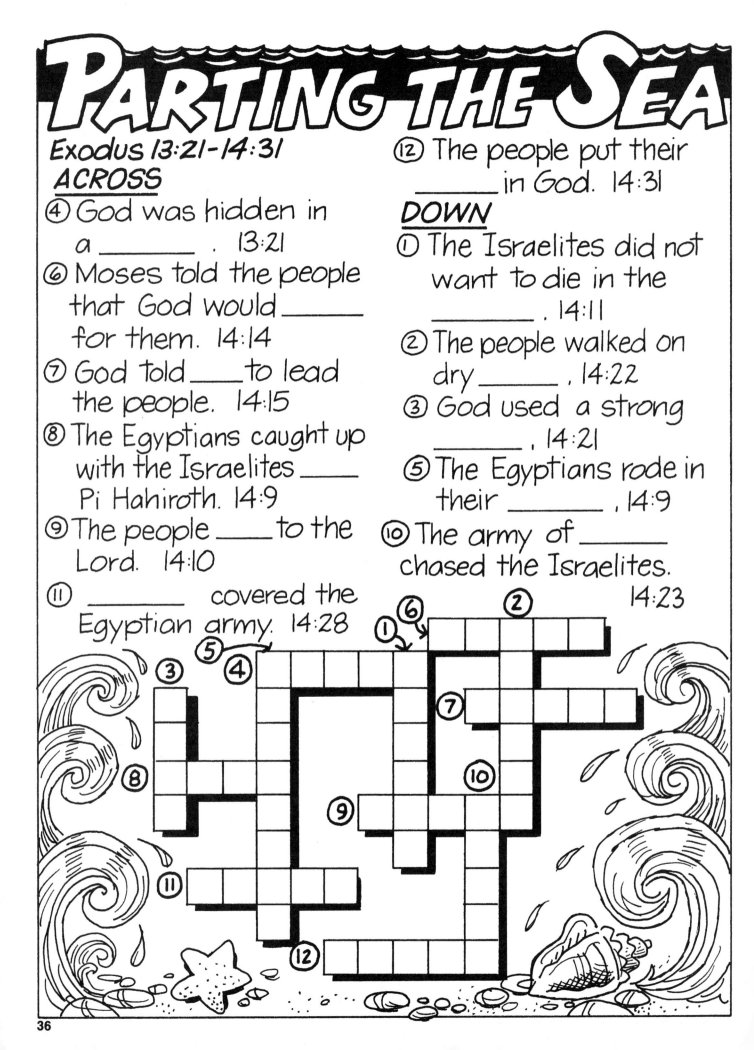

CREATION

Genesis 1-2: 23

God created...

Across
1 ... day and _____ . 1:5
2 ... dry ____ and the seas. 1:10
3 ... the garden called ____ . 2:8
4 ... the ___ to light the sky. 1:16

Down
5 ... all things in __ days. 1:31
6 ... plants and _____ . 1:12
7 ... man and _____ , 2:23
8 ... _____ in the sky. 1:21

5,000

One meal that fed

Read about this miracle in Mark 6:30-44.

Across

② A large _____ met Jesus on the shore. verse 34

④ Jesus and the apostles wanted to get some _____ . verse 31

⑥ Jesus told the disciples to give the crowd _____ , verse 37

⑧ Jesus _____ thanks for the food. verse 41

⑨ There _____ 12 baskets of food left over. verses 42,43

Down

① They took a ____ to find a quiet place. verse 32

③ The apostles wanted to ____ the crowd away. verse 36

⑤ They had _____ loaves and two fish. verse 38

⑦ All the people _____ and were full. verse 42

The Good Neighbor

Luke 10:25-37

Across

③ This story is called "The Parable of the _____ Samaritan."

⑤ A man _____ going to Jericho. verse 30

⑦ A _____ did not stop to help. verse 32

⑨ Robbers took the man's robe and _____ him. verse 30

Down

① A priest was on the same _____. verse 31

② The Samaritan gave the innkeeper two _____, verse 35

④ A Samaritan _____ to help the man who was hurt. verse 34

⑥ The _____ walked by. verse 31

⑧ The Samaritan took the man who was hurt to an _____. verse 34

Tax Man in a Tree

The story of Zacchaeus, told in Luke 19:1-10

Across

⑥ Zacchaeus wanted to _____ at Jesus.

⑦ He climbed into a fig _____.

⑧ _____ looked up and saw Zacchaeus.

⑨ Zacchaeus had a lot of _____.

⑩ Jesus called himself the ___ of man.

Down

① Zacchaeus said he would give ___ his money to the poor.

② Jesus went to Zacchaeus's _____.

③ Zacchaeus collected _____.

④ Jesus came to _____ sinners.

⑤ Jesus walked into the ____ _____ of Jericho.

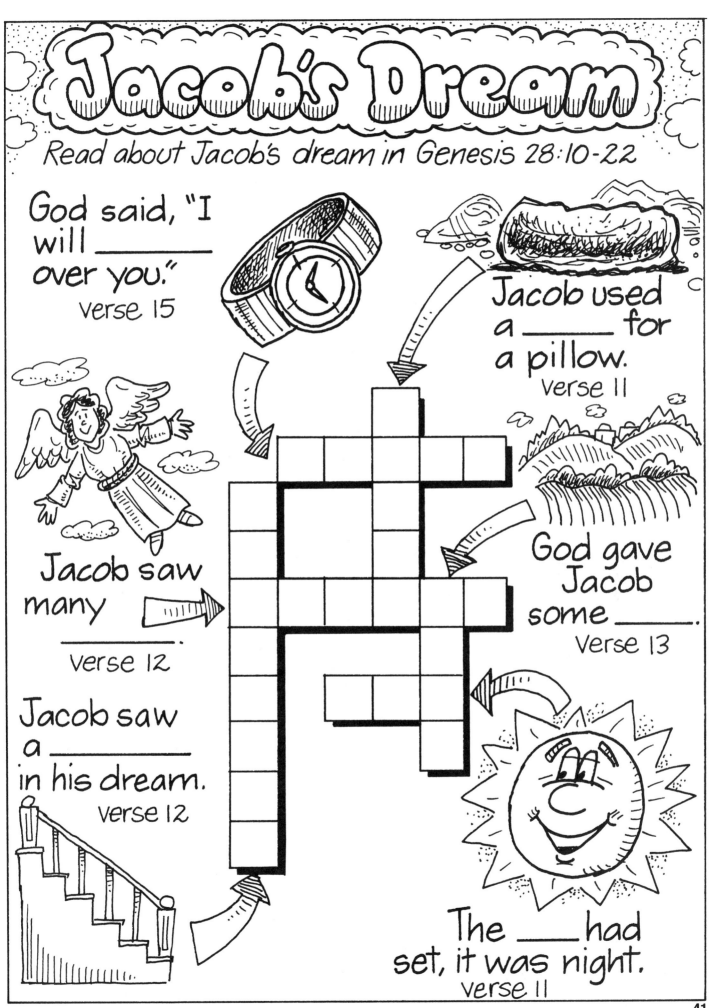

Jacob's Dream

Read about Jacob's dream in Genesis 28:10-22

God said, "I will _____ over you."
verse 15

Jacob used a _____ for a pillow.
verse 11

Jacob saw many _____.
verse 12

God gave Jacob some _____.
verse 13

Jacob saw a _____ in his dream.
verse 12

The _____ had set, it was night.
verse 11

CHAPTER 4 "PICTURE CLUES"

MAZES

IN A MAZE, YOU MUST FOLLOW THE CORRECT OPEN PATH IN ORDER TO GO FROM START TO FINISH.

TRY THESE MAZES

① THE LOST SHEEP
② THE LOST SON RETURNS
③ LET YOUR LIGHT SHINE!

HIDDEN PICTURES

EACH PAGE HAS LOTS OF STUFF HIDDEN IN THE PICTURE! SEE IF YOU CAN FIND ALL THE HIDDEN ITEMS LISTED FOR YOU.

① JOSEPH AND HIS BROTHERS
② NOAH BUILDS AN ARK
③ LOAVES AND FISHES

PICTURE CLUES

SOLVE THESE PUZZLES USING THE PICTURE CLUES
① 5TH COMMANDMENT
② MASTERS & SERVANTS
③ PENTECOST
④ HEAVEN IS LIKE...

REBUS

A REBUS IS A PUZZLE IN WHICH PICTURES STAND FOR WORDS. FIGURE OUT WHAT THE PICTURES "SAY", ADD OR SUBTRACT LETTERS AND BUILD BIBLE VERSES.

① MATTHEW 6:19 ② JAMES 4:8 ③ PROVERBS 18:10 ④ ISAIAH 40:8

THE LOST SHEEP

Help the shepherd find the lost sheep, and return it to the corral! Work your way through the maze from the shepherd, to the sheep, to the corral. Luke 15:3-7

STOP HERE

START HERE

THE LOST SON RETURNS

Can you help the lost son find his way back home to his family? After you are done, read the story in Luke 15:11-32.

Let your Light Shine!

Finish the verse by going through the lantern maze. Pick up letters as you go and write them below.

Start

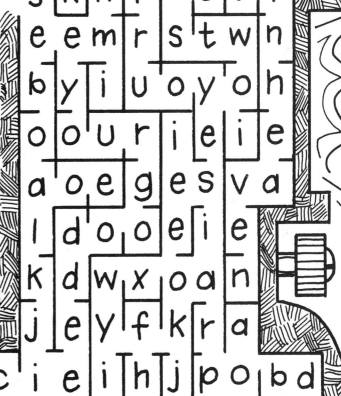

Matthew 5:16
"Let your light shine before men, that they may...

_____

_____

_____

JOSEPH AND HIS BROTHERS IN EGYPT

JOSEPH'S BROTHERS ARE LEAVING EGYPT FOR THE SECOND TIME. THEY BOUGHT GRAIN TO FEED THEIR FAMILIES. SEE IF YOU CAN FIND THESE THINGS HIDDEN BELOW- **20** SACKS OF GRAIN, **1** SILVER CUP AND THE NAMES OF ALL **11** BROTHERS. (HINT: THE SACK LOOKS LIKE THIS→)

LOAVES AND FISHES

IT WAS A MIRACLE! WITH ONLY 5 LOAVES OF BREAD AND 2 FISH, JESUS FED OVER 5,000 PEOPLE! SEE IF YOU CAN FIND **20** LOAVES AND **20** FISHES HIDDEN BELOW:

5th COMMANDMENT

Exodus 20:12

Name each picture. Write the first letter of each picture name on the line. Find out why we should obey the 6th Commandment.

SO THAT YOU MAY

             IN

THE LAND THE LORD

IS GIVING YOU.

Masters and Servants

John 13:1-17

Find out why Jesus washed the disciples' feet. Start with box A. Put the first letter of the picture in that box on the first line below. Then do the same with boxes B to Z.

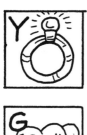

Jesus washed the disciples' feet to teach them this lesson:

Y ___ ___ ___ ___ ___ ___ B ___
A B   C D E F   G

___ ___ S ___ ___ ___ ___ ___ Y ___
H I J   K L M   N O   P Q

___ ___ ___ O ___ ___ ___ ___ ___ .
R S T   V W X Y Z

PENTECOST

Find out how we can receive the Holy Spirit! (Acts 2:38)

Name each picture. Write the first letter of each picture name on the line.

_____ _____ _____ _____ _____ _____
      AND BE

_____ _____ _____ _____ _____ _____ _____ _____

IN THE _____ _____ _____ _____

OF _____ _____ _____ _____ _____

THE KINGDOM OF HEAVEN IS LIKE...

Use the picture clue to finish each sentence. Heaven is like...

...a _ _ _ _ .
Matthew 13:47

...a man who planted good
_ _ _ _ _ .
Matthew 13:24-30

...a _ _ _ _ _ _ who prepared a wedding feast.
Matthew 22:2

..._ _ _ _ _ _ that a woman mixed into flour.
Matthew 13:33

..._ _ _ _ _ _ hidden in a field.
Matthew 13:44

...the owner of a
_ _ _ _ _ .
Matthew 13:52

52

TREASURES

1. ◯-NUT
2. ♪-e store
3. ☕-C
4. 🦶-ot + r
5. Y + 4 - F + selves   treasures
6. 1 - e
7. 👂 + th
8. W + ♥ - at + e
9. mo + 🐱 - ca + H
10. 🧵 - C + D
11. 🥜 - g + St
12. 🗄 k + 🚚 -uck + oy

Write answers
on these lines...

1. _____ 2. _____ store 3. _____ 4. _____
5. _____ treasures 6. __ 7. ____ , 8. ____
9. _____ 10. _____ 11. _____ 12. _____.

Matthew 6:19

53

REBUS James 4:8

① [comb] -b+e   ② n+ [ear]?

③ 2-w God   ④ [hand] -h

⑤ 3-tre   ⑥ w+[capsule]-p

⑦ [cow] -w+me   ⑧ n+♥-ht

⑨ Two-w   ⑩ [horseshoe]

① _____ ② _____ ③ _____

God ④ _____ ⑤ _____ ⑥ _____

⑦ _____ ⑧ _____ ⑨ _____ ⑩ _____ .

REBUS

1. T + [shoe] - so
2. n + [frame] - fr

of the

3. L + [knife] - sw
4. [lips] - lp
5. [axe] - xe
6. [star] - a + [ice cream cone] - ce + g
7. t + [flower] - fl

1. _____ 2. _____ of
the 3. _____ 4. _____ 5. _____
6. _____ 7. _____ .

Proverbs 18:10

~REBUS~

Isaiah 40:8

The 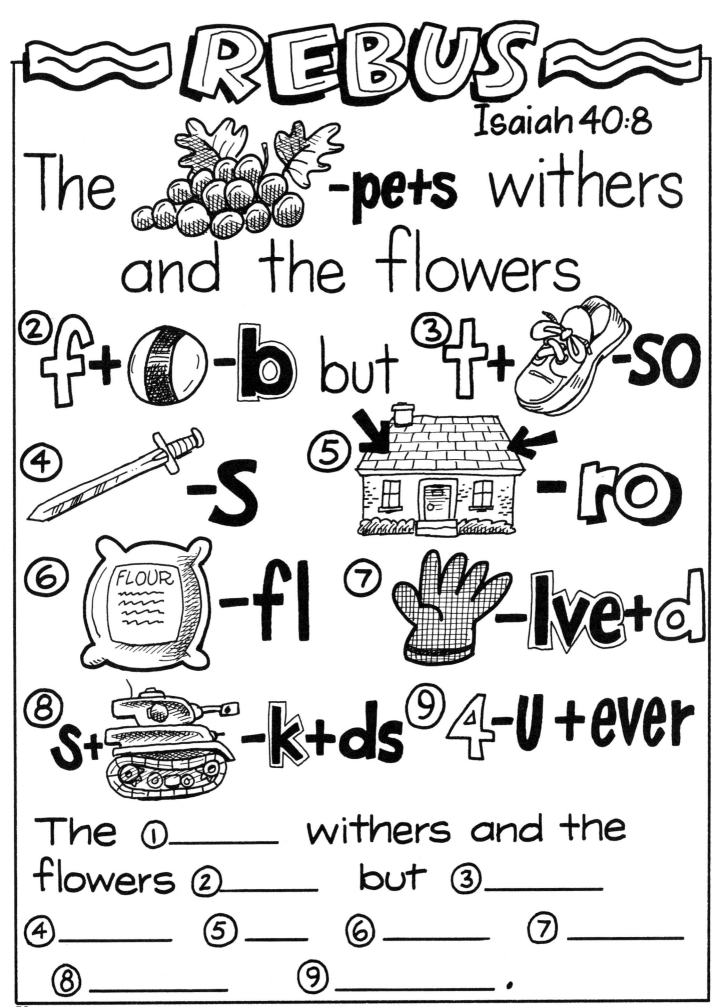-pets withers

and the flowers

② f+ ◯-b but ③ ✝+👟-so

④ 🗡-s ⑤ 🏠-ro

⑥ FLOUR-fl ⑦ 🧤-lve+d

⑧ s+🪖-k+ds ⑨ 4-U+ever

The ①＿＿＿ withers and the
flowers ②＿＿＿ but ③＿＿＿
④＿＿＿ ⑤＿＿＿ ⑥＿＿＿ ⑦＿＿＿
⑧＿＿＿ ⑨＿＿＿.

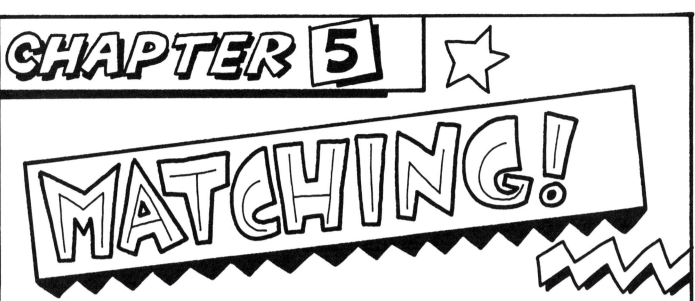

CHAPTER 5 ☆

MATCHING!

"MATCHING" MEANS CONNECTING 2 THINGS THAT ARE ALIKE. IT MIGHT BE A WORD AND A PICTURE OR A PERSON AND THEIR CORRECT NAME. SEE IF YOU CAN SOLVE THESE MATCHING BRAIN TEASERS:

① DISCIPLES
② WOMEN OF THE BIBLE
③ ALL KINDS OF ANIMALS
④ HEADLINES
⑤ JESUS HELPED...

KIDS! LOOK→ ANSWERS!

THE ANSWERS FOR EACH CHAPTER ARE ON THE LAST 2 PAGES OF THE BOOK.

GOOD LUCK!

Disciples

Match the disciples on the right with the correct facts on the left.

I was chosen to replace Judas Iscariot.
Acts 1:26

John

I tried to walk on water.
Matthew 14:29

Andrew

I was the only disciple to see Jesus on the cross.
John 19:26

Jesus saw me under a fig tree.
John 1:47-48

Thomas

I was a tax collector before becoming a disciple.
Matthew 10:3

Judas

Jesus told me to stop doubting and believe.
John 20:27

Peter

I was there when Jesus fed 5,000 people.
John 6:8

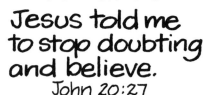
Matthew

Nathanael

I was the treasurer for the disciples.
John 12:4-6

Matthias

WOMEN OF THE BIBLE

Can you name these women? Use the clues to find out who they are.

I found out Samson's secret!

Judges 16:4-20

_ _ _ _ _ _ _

I was tending sheep when I met my husband Jacob.

Genesis 29:6

_ _ _ _ _ _

Jesus told me about the living water.

John 4:4-7

woman of

_ _ _ _ _ _ _

My mother-in-law was Naomi. I married Boaz.

_ _ _ _

I gave thanks to God when I saw the baby Jesus in the temple.

Luke 2:36-38

_ _ _ _

I am the mother of Jesus.

Matthew 1:18

_ _ _ _

Rachel   Samaria
Anna   Delilah   Mary   Ruth

ALL KINDS OF ANIMALS

Answer the questions below by drawing a line to the correct animal pictures. Use the rhyming clues to help you choose the right answers.

① Moses' rod became a _____.
   (Rhymes with ) Exodus 4:3

② God filled Egypt with _____.
   (Rhymes with) Exodus 8:6

③ _____ are small but very wise. Proverbs 30:24-25
   (Rhymes with)

④ The Israelites ate ___ in the wilderness.
   (Rhymes with) Exodus 16:13

⑤ Jesus sent the disciples to preach to the lost ___ of Israel.
   (Rhymes with) Matthew 10:5-6

⑥ In heaven, Jesus will divide the sheep and the _____.
   (Rhymes with) Matthew 25:31-33

⑦ A big ___ swallowed Jonah.
   (Rhymes with) Jonah 1:17

☆Headlines!☆

Draw a line from the headline to the person it describes:

Man builds big boat on dry land!

Young boy kills giant

Man spends night in lions' den!

Boy sold by his brothers!

Man parts the Red Sea!

Couple kicked out of garden for eating fruit!

Blind man knocks down temple!

12-year-old boy debates teachers in temple!

Noah
Genesis 6:13-14

Jesus
Luke 2:46-47

Adam and Eve
Genesis 3:23

Moses
Exodus 14:21

Joseph
Genesis 37:28

Daniel
Daniel 6:16-23

David
I Samuel 17:24,50

Samson
Judges 16:26-30

JESUS HELPED...

Use the clues to find out whom Jesus helps every day!

The 	Thirsty John 4:10
The 	Sick Mark 1:34
The 	Hungry Luke 9: 13-17
The 	Blind Mark 10:51-52
The 	Naked Luke 8:27,35
The 	Prisoner Matthew 11: 2-4
The 	Lost Luke 19:10

CHAPTER 1

TRIVIA <u>BIRTH OF JESUS</u> ①LUKE 2:3-5 ②LUKE 2:7 ③LUKE 1:26-31 ④MATTHEW 2:11 ⑤MATTHEW 2:8 ⑥LUKE 2:10 ⑦LUKE 2:36-38
<u>SLEEPERS</u> ①JESUS ②SAMSON ③PETER ④PHAROAH ⑤JACOB ⑥ADAM
<u>MIRACLES</u> ①PETER ②WATER ③TO HELP THEIR FRIEND ④5 ⑤PUT MUD ON HIS EYES ⑥HE BROUGHT HIM BACK TO LIFE
<u>CARING</u>...①WE SHOULD HONOR THEM ②RUTH ③GOD ④IF WE LOVE ONE ANOTHER ⑤WE SHOULD LOVE THEM ⑥POOR, LAME, ETC.
<u>JESUS ON THE CROSS</u> ①THIS IS THE KING OF THE JEWS ②SIMON ③IT STOPPED SHINING ④VINEGAR ⑤CRIMINALS ⑥JOSEPH

CHAPTER 2

JUMBLES <u>I SAMUEL 17:38-51</u> SLING·SWORD·ARMY·LORD·STICK
"GOD AND A ROCK"

<u>LUKE 4:1-13</u> STRIKE·STONE·FULL·YOUR·BECOME
"STRUCK OUT"

<u>I KINGS 3:5-14</u> WRONG·KING·SON·DREAM·YOU
"A WISE GUY"

<u>I KINGS 17:1-6</u> AHAB·HIDE·LORD·WORD·FEED
"BIRD FOOD"

<u>HOW TO PRAY</u> HEAVEN·NAME·COME·WILL·EARTH
BREAD·DEBTS·LEAD·EVIL

<u>ABSALOM</u> ① DAVID·ABSALOM·KING ② LEFT·AFRAID·SAD·DESERT ③ BATTLE·FOREST ④ MULE·OAK·HAIR·JOAB

<u>A WRESTLING MATCH</u> ① JACOB·BROTHER·ATTACK ② GOD·GIFTS·COWS·CAMELS·GOATS ③ RIVER·MAN·NIGHT·ASKED ④ BLESSED·NAME·KNEW

CODES <u>WHO IS JESUS?</u> HEALER·SAVIOR·TEACHER·JUDGE·KING·PERFECT·TRUTH·GRACE

<u>A NET FULL OF FISH</u> ANGELS WILL DIVIDE THE BAD FROM THE GOOD. THE BAD WILL BE THROWN INTO A FIERY FURNACE.
<u>JESUS PRAYED,,,</u> HILLS·TOMB·CROSS·TABLE·UPPER ROOM·RIVER
<u>BUILDING BARNS</u> · THINGS CANNOT SAVE US, GOD WILL NOT FAIL US!
<u>JERICHO</u> · SEVENTH · MARCH · PRIESTS · TRUMPETS · SHOUT · TUMBLE
<u>BLESSINGS</u> · HEAVEN · COMFORT · MERCY · GOD · SONS · HEAVEN

Answers continued on next page...

CHAPTER 3

CROSSWORD "JESUS IS BORN" ACROSS ①INN ②ANGEL ④BABY ⑦HOUSE ⑧CHRIST DOWN ②NAZARETH ⑤GOD ⑥BLESSED

"IN THE LION'S DEN" ACROSS ①DANIEL ⑤DARIUS ⑥SLEEP ⑧ANGEL ⑩TRUSTED DOWN ②TIMES ③LIONS ④PRAY ⑦RESCUE ⑨NOT ⑪GOD

"PARTING THE SEA" ACROSS ④CLOUD ⑥FIGHT ⑦MOSES ⑧NEAR ⑨CRIED ⑪WATER ⑫TRUST DOWN ①DESERT ②GROUND ③WIND ⑤CHARIOTS ⑩EGYPT

"CREATION" ACROSS①NIGHT ②GROUND ③EDEN ④STARS DOWN⑤SIX ⑥TREES ⑦WOMAN ⑧BIRDS

"ONE MEAL..." ACROSS ②CROWD ④REST ⑥FOOD ⑧GAVE ⑨WERE DOWN ①BOAT ③SEND ⑤FIVE ⑦ATE

"THE GOOD NEIGHBOR" ACROSS ③GOOD ⑤WAS ⑦LEVITE ⑨BEAT DOWN ①ROAD ②COINS ④WENT ⑥PRIEST ⑧INN

"TAX MAN IN A TREE" ACROSS ⑥LOOK ⑦TREE ⑧JESUS ⑨MONEY ⑩SON DOWN ①HALF ②HOUSE ③TAXES ④SAVE ⑤TOWN

CHAPTER 4

PICTURE CLUES ① 5TH COMMANDMENT · HONOR YOUR FATHER AND YOUR MOTHER, SO THAT YOU MAY LIVE LONG... ② MASTERS AND SERVANTS · YOU WILL BE BLESSED IF YOU HELP OTHERS. ③ PENTECOST · REPENT AND BE BAPTIZED IN THE NAME OF JESUS. ④ HEAVEN IS LIKE... A NET · A KING · SEED · YEAST · TREASURE · HOUSE

REBUS ① DO NOT STORE UP FOR YOURSELVES TREASURES ON EARTH, WHERE MOTH AND RUST DESTROY. ② COME NEAR TO GOD AND HE WILL COME NEAR TO YOU. ③ THE NAME OF THE LORD IS A STRONG TOWER. ④ THE GRASS WITHERS AND THE FLOWERS FALL BUT THE WORD OF OUR GOD STANDS FOREVER.

CHAPTER 5

MATCHING ①DISCIPLES (FROM TOP OF PAGE DOWN) MATHIAS · PETER · JOHN · NATHANAEL · MATTHEW · THOMAS · ANDREW · JUDAS

②WOMEN DELILAH · RACHEL · SAMARIA · RUTH · ANNA · MARY

③ANIMALS ①SNAKE ②FROGS ③ANTS ④QUAIL ⑤SHEEP ⑥GOATS ⑦FISH

④HEADLINES (LEFT TO RIGHT) NOAH DAVID DANIEL JOSEPH MOSES ADAM &EVE SAMSON JESUS

⑤JESUS HELPED (FROM TOP OF PAGE DOWN) ·BLIND·THIRSTY· NAKED·LOST·SICK·HUNGRY·PRISONER